THE END

Skip Morrow

An Owl Book

Holt, Rinehart and Winston ● **New York**

For my wife, Laraine, and our child, unnamed.
I know exactly
where I want to be
in the end.

Copyright © 1983 by Skip Morrow

All rights reserved, including the right to reproduce this book or portions thereof in any form.
Published by Holt, Rinehart and Winston, 383 Madison Avenue, New York, New York 10017.
Published simultaneously in Canada by Holt, Rinehart and Winston of Canada, Limited.

Library of Congress Catalog Card Number: 82-83314
ISBN: 0-03-063401-6
First Edition

Printed in the United States of America
1 3 5 7 9 10 8 6 4 2

ISBN 0-03-063401-6

1.

2.

3.

4.